★ Kristi Yamaguchi ★

PHOTO CREDITS
Allsport USA
Mike Powell: Cover and pg. 18.
Tim DeFrisco: pg. 2, 10, 14, 29 and 30. Bernard Asset: pg. 6.
Bob Martin: pg. 9, 17, 22 and 26. George Vandystadt: pg. 13 and 25.
Jean-Marc Loubat: pg. 21.

Distributed to Schools and Libraries
in the United States by
ENCYCLOPAEDIA BRITANNICA CORP.
310 S. Michigan Avenue
Chicago, Illinois 60604

Library of Congress Catalog-in-Publication Data
Rambeck, Richard
Kristi Yamaguchi / Richard Rambeck.
p. cm.
Summary: A biography of the young ice skater who won the gold medal
in women's figure skating in the 1992 Olympics.
ISBN 1-56766-071-1
1. Yamaguchi, Kristi–Juvenile literature. 2. Skaters–United States–
Biography–Juvenile literature. [1. Yamaguchi, Kristi.
2. Ice skaters. 3. Japanese Americans–Biography.]
I. Title.
GV850.Y36R36 1994   92-43058
796.91'092–dc20   CIP/AC
[B]

★ Kristi Yamaguchi ★

by Richard Rambeck

Yamaguchi at the medals platform.

Thered she was at last in Albertville, France, waiting for the women's figure-skating medals to be awarded in the 1992 Winter Olympics. And Kristi Yamaguchi had no idea what she should do. In all her years of skating practice, she had never practiced this moment. Did she have to say anything? That's what she leaned over and asked her friend and roommate for the last two weeks, Nancy Kerrigan. No, Nancy assured her, Kristi didn't have to say a word. All she had to do was wait until they called her name. Then she would skate out to the platform, climb to the top level, and let them drape the gold medal around her shoulders.

Not many people expected Yamaguchi to win the gold medal in women's figure skating in the 1992 Olympics. Yamaguchi thought her best chance would be at the 1994 Games in Lillehammer, Norway. After all, the 1992 Games were her first Olympics, and she was only twenty years old. When Yamaguchi left for France, she just wanted to do her best. Most people expected Midori Ito from Japan to win the gold medal. Yamaguchi and U.S. teammate Tonya Harding both hoped they would win medals—possibly even the gold—but they did not expect to.

When Yamaguchi arrived in France, she decided to enjoy the Olympic experience as much as she could. She went to the opening ceremonies and stayed in the Olympic village. But she was not able to get enough time to practice on the ice, so she and her coach, Christy Ness, drove to an ice rink thirty-five miles away. Yamaguchi, who was a little worried that she had lost her touch, found it at the practice rink, away from all the crowds. "She skated beautifully," Ness said. "Prettier than anything I've seen."

After Yamaguchi
finished that special practice, her
coach sat her down and said,
"That's all. You don't have to try
to do anything more than what
you just did. If you skate like
that, it doesn't matter what else
happens." Ness told Yamaguchi
just to skate, just to enjoy herself
on the ice. If Yamaguchi had been
getting a little nervous, this
relaxed her. She and Ness
returned to Albertville. Even
today, Ness recalls that practice
session: "It was so beautiful, it
didn't matter if a panel of judges
put her second."

12

With millions of people watching, the women's figure-skating competition started, and the tension was high. Both Ito and Harding fell during their short programs. The other skaters all seemed nervous on the ice except Yamaguchi and her roommate, Nancy Kerrigan, both of the United States. Indeed, Yamaguchi skated her way to first place in the short program, which counted for one-third of the total score. If she skated well in the long program, too, she would win the gold medal. Perhaps she got butterflies in her stomach, because during her long program, Yamaguchi fell as she performed one of her jumps. A fall could destroy her chances. Luckily for her, all the other top skaters also had falls.

When the competition ended, Yamaguchi was first, Ito was second, and Kerrigan was third. Yamaguchi had won the gold medal. "It's something I've dreamed of ever since I put on skates as a little girl," she said. When Yamaguchi was young, she wanted to be like U.S. skater Dorothy Hamill, who won the Olympic figure-skating gold medal in 1976. But Yamaguchi had been born clubfooted—her feet were twisted and she had to wear special shoes to correct them. The shoes must have done their job, because Yamaguchi started to skate at the age of six.

18

Yamaguchi grew up in Fremont, California, near Oakland. Her father, Jim, was a dentist, and her mother, Carole, was a medical secretary. Both Yamaguchi parents encouraged their three children to get involved in sports. Lori, the oldest, was a member of a championship baton-twirling team. Brett, the youngest, was a fine basketball player. For Kristi, though, the only sport was figure skating. While Kristi was in high school, her mother would wake up before 4:00 in the morning so she could drive Kristi to the ice rink by 5:00.

Christy Ness started coaching Kristi Yamaguchi when Yamaguchi was ten. Unlike most people in the sport, Yamaguchi skated both singles and pairs. That meant she had to practice her singles routine and then turn around and skate with a partner. In other words, Yamaguchi had to work twice as hard as most skaters. "I don't think she ever thinks of being tired," Ness said. "But with her schedule, she couldn't." The work paid off, because Yamaguchi soon became one of the top junior skaters—in both singles and pairs—in the country.

At the 1989 U.S. Championships, Yamaguchi showed the nation what she could do—in both singles and pairs. She and her partner Rudy Galindo won the pairs competition. Then Yamaguchi amazed even herself and her coach by finishing second in singles, placing behind two-time champion Jill Trenary. She became the first woman in thirty-five years to win medals in both of the two events at the U.S. Championships. And this "woman" was only seventeen years old. Her height was four feet and eleven inches, and her weight was just eighty-two pounds.

Yamaguchi was now one of the top singles skaters in the world. But because she was still a pairs skater, too, she only practiced her singles routine about half as much as the other top skaters. "She's superhuman," said her pairs coach, Jim Hulick. Yamaguchi teamed with Galindo to win the U.S. pairs championship again in 1990. But after that, she decided to compete only in singles. Even though she and Galindo were the top U.S. pair, they weren't one of the best in the world.

The best hope of success for Yamaguchi was not in pairs. She was becoming one of the best singles skaters on the planet. In 1989, when Yamaguchi first made a splash as a singles skater, she was known as an outstanding jumper. Despite her small size, she had powerful muscles that could propel her high in the air. "Where does she get her strength?" asked one official of the United States Figure Skating Association. "I've got houseplants that are thicker than her legs."

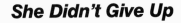

Even though she now rehearsed singles only, Yamaguchi had a tough time reaching the top among U.S. skaters. During the 1991 U.S. Championships, Jill Trenary suffered an injury, and that seemed to open the door for Yamaguchi to win her first singles title. Tonya Harding won instead. Yamaguchi could have become depressed or put herself down, but that wasn't her style. "On Kristi's most frustrating days, she shows it—maybe—but only in her body language," Ness explained. "That's all."

It's hard to reach the top.

Yamaguchi's frustration ended at the 1991 World Championships. Her patience was paying off: She finally won her first women's singles title, beating Harding and Ito. In early 1992, she skated to the U.S. singles championship. A month later, she added the Olympic gold medal to her trophy case. At age twenty, Yamaguchi had become the top woman skater in the world. "Kristi has the ideal attitude for a skater," said U.S. skating coach Don Laws. "She trusts her coach, her parents, and her program." That trust—and talent and hard work—just might win her another gold medal in 1994.

475150

jB
YAMAGUCH
I

Rambeck, Richard

Kristi Yamaguchi

$14.95

DATE			